T0366045

The Myth of Being

ELIZABETH CLAYTON

Order this book online at www.trafford.com
or email orders@trafford.com

Most Trafford titles are also available at major online book retailers.

 www.trafford.com

North America & international
toll-free: 1 888 232 4444 (USA & Canada)
fax: 812 355 4082

Our mission is to efficiently provide the world's finest, most comprehensive book publishing service, enabling every author to experience success. To find out how to publish your book, your way, and have it available worldwide, visit us online at www.trafford.com

ISBN: 978-1-4907-9937-7 (sc)
ISBN: 978-1-4907-9936-0 (e)

Print information available on the last page.

Trafford rev. 01/14/2020

Contents

The first knowledge that I have of knowing life with thought
was in my third year, before memory.

All I have is a passing impression which has been with me all my years.

As an omniscient observer, I saw myself crawling under a barbed wired fence,
others beside, known only by sense of presence; and I saw the skirt of navy
blue with small white flowers that dress material of humble people of that
period; falling into and moving in the material, were bright red apples.

This image became my first captured, in the cover of this
work, my first verse: the myth of being. -

Stemmed Day

Within the salutation of morning,

A day, and beautiful, upon a stem,

Its petal colors bright,

Shaped to the pattern most pleasing, softly round:

About it hangs the fragrance of widest,

Bluest sky,

And inside its center, intense joy,

So that I stood with Moses,

And could not look into its fullest fire;

Passing were other blossoms,

Dreams that flew away into unimportant musings.

How beautiful, this day upon a stem;

Let my instrument of gathering be strong and powerful,

And my the forgiven flower's life move in eager folds,

In majesty suiting the chosen,

The blood of the seed,

Down to the earth,

Before its quieted splendor:

In my hand the day,

Its beauty and generosity above all,

And first, of all else,

That can be given.

-A verse written some ten years ago, but metaphor, true, to this record (day) of my thoughts into verse at their beginning until today *The Myth of Being*

First Season

In the matter of being rests its premier portion,

That of becoming;

And we must to know the beauty of this recognition.

In place, then, lies the past, vestiges of various tenses:

Of then and now, of soon and late,

The entire repertoire of yesterday and memory.

Beside is found the future, its expectations and firstness,

Energy, closeted, the mystical, the clouded worlds

Of dreams and visions.

But most, we find the moment – our present:

Revisiting – to view, again, the plains of Carthage;

Resolving- one with Francesca's tryst

Of the carnal and the spiritual; looking at what is,

And harvesting its gold, in the fiery passion of now.

There is, in these, all, - most, perhaps,

To be found in the moment – immediacy –

If at times with a stretching out –

But all seasons of traversment –

That toward – into a kind of stillness,

Of which we can find the fabric of awareness.

In this lovely – absolutely magnificent – fan of opening reality

We don our splendid hues, and formulate our grande,

And small importances;

We construct the individual buttresses our souls

Require for the remaining – but, truly, the only movement,

Flowing – as it is left, ever,

Our forward movement – that into our own,

Our personal eternity.

Sunday, January 5, 2014

-Alone, hard cold coming; a true winter day in these Southern climes – a spontaneous piece, with no thought, before – conscious, that is – only grim personal arrangements –

Dedication

To my brothers, my little brown skins,

Who, with my parents before and along with me –

became the beautiful summers, their\our myths :

Wayne

Marion

David

Foreword

There are individuals one meets in life that allow the expanding of his horizons, to see the beauty in the world, and force the examination of the sacred in life, in his own life and in others. Elizabeth Clayton is such a person. She is brilliant, artistic, contemplative, inspiring and vibrant, all the while maintaining her humility. Her life has been a collage of experiences that have given her the sensitivity to look beyond the mundane, and understand the rich colors and profound thoughts that inspire those she teaches. She draws Art and Literature together in a beautiful way -- be prepared to be inspired.

John W. Norton, M. D.
May 20, 2014

Acknowledgments

When brought completely, a flower is usually composed, beautifully, into a center, and many lovely petals, these attached to the center, and it to a stem. The stem is necessary, but not as beauty, particularly, but necessary to the flower's being. The stem can be compared to the larger "feeding" portion of a published work, the support of the community through education and other avenues of strength, that of family and friendships, beside.

Finally, the petals are numerous, with full recognition and will, within, outward to the center, the composing essential; but the petals close to the center, need special recognition – and so I offer my greatest expression of gratitude to my physician and friend, my mentor in every good manner, Dr. John Norton, of the University of Mississippi Medical Center, Jackson, MS, who also has prepared the foreword to this most recent work. And by my side, my assistant, Tonia Germany, who takes care to all to all technical matters, as all matters in getting a manuscript to its destination; the publishing process, itself. These two, a lovely duet, have joined my efforts toward publication of this, my earliest verse. I am indebted immeasurably, and with sincerest gratitude.

Elizabeth
Spring 2014

Preface

To

The Myth of Being

A holistic view, of any matter, is requiring, and in no wise is the combined sentiment of the verse of my intimate childhood experiences included in this present volume, and the effective execution of its written description, different. The verses which have been presented in this most recently published work are both prelude and conclusion to the entire of my compositions, until the present; they record the very first of my "songs," entering so long ago, that there is no record of them, other than the daily visitation of various of them inside my heart. "When one is a child, he speaks as a child" (acts\behaves)...to put away childish things when he is older. But children are capable of more than speaking, and acting- much more – they also feel, and not obviously, as primitively or elementarily as they may speak or act – for the apparatus governing emotion is older, more able – more as the heartbeat; it does not require instruction to function, or reminding to begin or conclude; neither is it so situationalistic (incomplete as to accuracy) that its products- feelings- necessarily be put away with other "childish" things. "Feeling," "emotion," "sentiment" – each of these words is very clouded as to origin and nourishment, so much so that such terms or included phrases, surprisingly, yet connote, if with struggle, what of reality can be perceived, regarding much of human relationships. Feelings do not require commands or need embrace practice, but are most, pure, or true, if spontaneous.

A first attempt at recording my earliest verses did occur in my twenties, but the pieces were set aside with the circumstances of my life, especially an unhappy second marriage, but most, an advancing, difficult period in Bipolar illness, this period extending into about twenty years when an effective mood stabilizer was found. These verses include my position in assessment held today, and speak my earliest, somewhat prophetic summation of life.

These earliest "songs" salute the gift of life, its beauty, and sadness, its steps into the journey, and all of the steps, following – until I became too ill to compose, if only in thought that may could have been pulled again into awareness when I was again well. But the night is not forever, and writing was, eventually, resumed. Perhaps one of my greatest regrets is the loss of twenty years, including the "slide" into, and the desperate efforts toward reorienting.

The experience of collecting, and preparing for publishing, these earliest of my verses, has brought pensive moments which offer reflection into the whole of my life, my thought – including the years following the concluding verses in this present volume. I find, then, some necessity to comment on the full of my compositions, for *The Myth of Being* encompasses the complete of my thought – a microcosm of the years, all, following: subjects, ideas, and modes of description/presentation – together with the inside questions, those which have, by their press, colored all of my hours.

Childhood is innocent, but this quality does not prevent the seeing or learning of truth; if such truth is uncomfortable, yet in instances, wounding – or simply pressing – avenues are chosen to help address these truths, other than avenues which may appear more "natural," or age appropriate; questioning, acting, reflecting and, ultimately, choosing occur, as can, also, denial or fanciful maneuvers. At the least, a heaviness often falls about, an intensity, these offering, also, an exquisite beauty.

I write, then, of the subject of early childhood –young adulthood - emotion – feelings – as I hold a newly gathered blossom – very tenuously. With information can come more understanding, and I would hope to invite those who have already read my verse to listen now, to its prefacing. This, my work, is without any effort toward pretense, praise, or any secondary gain – only the joy, the need to express in its firstness.

To begin, I step into a time of far away, into distant yesterday, since at the first remembrance of "things past," the distance is real. There was not accomplishment enough, in the use of words, to describe, in any acceptable fashion, the several events and circumstances that I experienced, truly, before memory was open to me, or think to care for recording. And so, remaining, earlier, are mere impressions, often with the appointments of sound and fragrance – in audible silence, a pattern woven into a portion of fabric; punctuating the silence were the droning songs of summer locusts, in the rural; and found, also, lovely images which spring from the larger natural such as the colors of the rainbow, dressing a longed for, "Sunday" garment.

A move, at about ten years of age, was, perhaps, the deciding factor in my full attempt to adjust properly, putting the fanciful in place and accepting a reality which I knew I could probably not accept. I began writing at just this time, diaries, short stories, and some verse, suggesting what were, or would have been to the trained eye, serious symptoms. Having always lived in the rural, I was now inside a small city where my parents were to achieve their higher education so that they could go into ministerial work; I was, in the years of early puberty, without friends, with new challenges and competition, as well as almost poverty in my home – and all that such a condition brings with it. But my will was strong, as was my body, and I continued to achieve, and write – bits and pieces, and no longer images alone.

The small number of verses of this collection were honest attempts to try and escape, or make more beautiful, that which wounded my sensibilities. I was not yet four years of age when the first images impressed; the existence of my family, until I had graduated high school, did not alter enough to afford the comfort my spirit required – neither then, nor in the years following.

I was sensitive to the natural as a comfort, but as constant as it was, the conflicts of my family, negative circumstances I did not fully understand, nor the whole of this dynamic, pushed me more toward the wielding power of beauty, in the arts, academic excellence, personal attractiveness, and interest in all areas of love, and freedom – any positive movement, in my perception, away from strife. These factors, all, find presence in calling up earlier attempts to secure a kind escape. Therefore, all images recorded as a young adult suggest this principle – during the slow, but deliberate progression of my illness into its flowering, and debilitation; this feature draped the preordained unfolding of my person.

Through another manner of expression, words from the advanced cognition of a trained and seasoned, matron woman, I entered, dependent, with qualities developmentalists now taunt as advanced, creative, knowing. Such information can only be documented in the playing out through the developmental process – a dependent, helpless physical and mental self on the threshold of being, now truly to be advanced toward thought, to reason, its abstractions and its review. I have memories, more impressions, since before age four; they are so distant, as to particulars, so that only sounds, fragrance and such illicit their invitation. It is from this point, this avenue of departure, that I literally plunged into the stream of life – being; it was a wonderland that I perceived, one which, because of my beginning, or predisposition to illness, I constructed to be a season of beauty.

As children, together with our parents, we lived in poor, isolated, rural circumstances in Mississippi, following the Great Depression in our country, and the second great "world" war which, eventually, saw our people out of both, unhappy colorings. In this setting, we lived humbly, simply, innocently; however, such circumstances did not prevent intellectual and spiritual development and growth, beside play and creative activities. Unhappy experiences within our home, though softened by genuine love and care, played out our parents' early lives – poverty, abandonment and abuse, lack of educational opportunities, and their accompanying positive attributes. Questioning was our fare, with a measure of mourning.

The solitude of our rural separateness as children will always image a kind of peace to me, if surrounded at times by loneliness. There were my three brothers, my little "brownskins," and my parents, my mother, chronically ill of depression and other symptomatic arrangements, and my father, passionate, strong but tender, a quality he covered in order to maintain control with his strength. Some of these earliest images and impressions are not well understood, even after all of the years of courting what secrets of good they might carry: apples being thrown, and being caught – these into a woman's full, long skirt, while she was seated; and crawling, carefully under a barbed wire fence, very close to the soil, cattle nearby, my companions known to be with me, but shadowed so that their identities remain unknown.

I have written of that I remember, when I became a young adult, hovering close, almost to the full expression of the illness which has kept me in its clasp, all of my days. I remember, and I have "said" of these matters: friend and kin, especially to my nuclear family were never in our presence; later, however, there are those, colleagues and such, true, and not so much so, and a small number of friends who have been in circle since the early years, to include my two long-term psychiatrists, beginning in my mid-twenties, extending into the present; finally, waits my truest, most giving friend, always in its complete – the grande Natural, a presence – the very "face of God" – a constant presence; these also have been beside, biding: grave ponderings within myself.

My world as a small child was "small," narrow, in some sense, but truly broad inside an unchangeable world view which played out as seeing the world, despite my fundamentalist instruction, without a great deal of judgmental trappings. My world was different, but in its particulars, a "wealthy bare" -but it was difficult - on many fronts, in a manner that escapes, for repair, the wisdom of a child.

Family, school, church – these filled my life with wonder and joy, alongside the awareness of natural will, private wanderings, and yearnings for other beauty, these to augment the difficult, if simple, safe, and uncomplicated.

I knew that a larger world existed – outside our humble fences, out of reach or touch and description – except through small readings at school. These such avenues fired my curiosity and the need to pursue, although my love of solitude, and my thoughts, were a great companion, aside. Imaginary pictures of any subject of attention, then, grew into remembrance; these are movement within my work, and they will remain. The perceptual process involved throughout my childhood would be a discussion prohibitive, but I will add a conversation, possible. I was probably a child with tender temperament, having a pre-Bipolar fancifulness; I was quite bright, able, and, being fanciful, brought into myself a fanciful world, dark moods ushering in when this routine failed. My natural state of innocence was intensified by the awakening illness, and the cohorts of time and place, historically, added to the balance problem as I grew into pubescence.

I reeled under the precocious visitation of puberty and full, abstract thought, alone in "disorder and early sorrow." Darkness soon became my fare, beside the light. Intra-familial circumstances called out a love and devotion as deep as the fundamentalist religious doctrine we children were taught, bringing a dissonance with my emerging curiosities and need for the excitement of the new and intensely beautiful.

Much energy and spontaneity were lost, but we each felt the joy, the promise of life, these to increase with our parents' decision to leave the rural and return to school and church ministry.

I can only express gratitude for the all years of my life, to know now, today, that "being" is a myth in the larger sense – of living fully, abundantly, with gifts and giving, to only become a reality to those who, each in his own fashion, endures the "struggle" of "true becoming." In it all, I am only grateful for the adventure – of great fulfillment – these poor images, perhaps calling forth roses, garlands and oxen – these – brought into existence and form by maturity in various areas of endeavor and careful thought. And I cannot agree more, with the early modern, Russian author,

Anton Chekhov, in his assessment of the true weltanschauung of most individuals: that life is a gray, dreary affair, from which we depart, often, for a better experience – anything – a meal, a gift, a holiday, an illicit tryst – frantically we pour over the possibilities. Most, as per Chekhov, do not observe that there is a possible feast, and they do not go to table, often or long. Perhaps this concept underlies the frantic, empty busyness which characterizes our overall approach to life – certainly in these, our Western cultures. Rouses are often successful – in replacing the clarity we fear.

With gratitude embracing all of my years, I feel that each of us as children, my brothers, has realized his myth, in separate, different fashions. I wished, as distantly as I can give thought, to awake in the morning- an absolute threshold to repeated joy, literally- and with that joy, leap into the stream – to go outside, as our parents allowed us, to see the new day: new growth, its life beside the death of yesterday's blossoms – more beauty, in some fashion, in decay without life. I wished the full day, to eat, to drink, all of it, to take into myself, the full feast. The intensity of these risings was, and in reflection, is, with me, yet – in my painting, sculpture, as well as writing. And the day must to often be, and has been, constructed to support my penchant for beauty. I live into the day, its adverse qualities, outward, and within myself; and I fall, exhausted, in conclusion, only to know the satisfaction I must experience. The turn is that we do not need "struggle" half our lives "to be"; we always have had potential and opportunity "to be, to become." Our years "in the wilderness" were a wealth of experience, receiving and giving; we learned and absorbed until the milieu for our expression required change. We lost, but gained, immeasurably. And, still, the saga continues; a distant point of attainment is not necessary. And peace is neither a certificate we earn inside a given circumstance, to be hung and admired; the moment, lived fully, is the arena of "being-" this is the "process," the "struggle," of "true becoming."

In childhood we realized that which was possible, and as we, with weeping, moved our fences out, beyond, into – we "became," again, more, and we continue. *"Being" is a cognizant stance we enjoy when we fulfill all, or some of our needs – as we are able to do so. Some regret may insist, but it is not the larger realization.* Acceptance, with gratitude, is the overpowering sentiment of my years, if there is the persistent mourning. The verses comprising this small volume reflect the joy and beauty of all of our lives, however despair has impinged upon them. Questions and acceptance can sit beside each other; the mind, masterfully, always protects itself, using whatever strategies will be effective, until they are no longer effective.

The much celebrated English poet, Robert Browning, may conclude my sentiments in a better fashion than I can voice them. In his verse, "Andrea del Sarto," there is a very recognizable line, "Ah, but a man's reach should exceed his grasp...." But I choose as his better line_ toward the conclusion of the piece, for its truth in this matter of "being" – summarily, for those who live with purpose and gratitude: "There strikes a balance."

"The child is father to the man."

William Wordsworth

The woundings in life cannot be put aside, completely,

To be without memory; their pain

is, in some measure, always.

But life's resplendent balming, beside, allows "getting past"

these pain, to see the glory of man's purpose and experience.

Beauty, of whatever variety, is a predominant balm,

And so we weep, but our joy lifts ever, upward.

The love of the grande Natural, of each other with faith

And the pleasuring of learning,

The richness of anticipation, effort, and accomplishment –

Inside able innocence –

These, all, dressed our earliest hours,

And we, together, "became."

First Voice

Note

The dates accompanying the verses are sometimes of their composition, but often only of their being formally made record. The verses are arranged into the text in the true order of composition, as memory allowed, with some few notations which were found with the originals.

First Memory

The first time I was,

I sat on the back doorsteps,

Polishing my new black patent leather shoes

With the last breakfast biscuit;

My new shoes had round toes and straps

And buckles across the arch.

I polished and Mamma talked, and then,

I dropped the biscuit and the chickens

Picked it up and ran away.

But Mamma's voice was still there.

The steps were wooden and rough, and seemed high.

She was saying that she was not well,

Not for a long time and would have to go away,

For a long time – and she did.

Age three –four,

Before my mother's hospitalization for a period of emotional illness -

Excerpt from *I, Elizabeth*

The seasons, in the rural, had each, its unique beauty, its special call to me. There were happy snatches from the grief—animals wood fires, heavy quilts, hand stitched, Christmas, Vacation Bible school, revivals; there was preparation for church, an almost frenzy of activity to look and be our best, and in the evenings, at home, family alter. The ebbing and flowing included small disasters, of course, and they touched me also: the unwanted pregnancy and accepted birth of my youngest brother, the ice storm of 1951 which required my father to continuously scavenge for wood to keep one fireplace affording heat; I remember his eyes, for he became snow-blind from the excessive glare of the light of day on snow all over, everywhere, for days. In all his chores, however, I remember his tender lessons, showing us how to catch and roast birds, a kind of happy, engaging activity pulled forth from the intolerable circumstance. (2007)

Early Royalty

It's sweet-olive time now

With the earliest daffodils,

Bent in the morning with the night's cold –

And the soft, crimson powder puff

Of camellia petals settled

Around their sturdy trunk.

Spring 1973

Winter

Winter came to me today.

I saw blackbirds fly and I felt the self

That walks behind the promenade of white puffs

Of chilled breath,

Whistling,

Along a silent, still path

To warm hearth-hours.

January 17, 1973

Cakewalk

Upturned,

Freckles lying against his shiny rose,

There was innocence and genuine trust,

And worth enough

To fill all that lay beyond the gate;

Dark became light

And sky touched the earth

In a smile.

At Beauregard, MS, before seventh grade,

And move out of the rural

Certainty

The prettiest pink I know is the first peach bloom,

Before the rivalry with its tender leaves,

Before the wilting from coming fruit.

-Just in time to assure (one) that,

Although viewed in cold,

Warm is near.

June 18, 1969

Play

The soil and a stick;

Playfulness and laughter

And voila,

There is a circle and a game.

The marble is in our hands

And we can move it;

And if we do not score

We are advised of the shooter,

And so stand strong in our certitude.

But that is not always the way;

Yet we continue to shoot,

Leaning forward

As we touch and move.

A beautiful memory –

With my brothers, as children

Written after 1992

Brought Back

Leaving the wealth of late summer dreams,

I can smell and taste again cold, set coffee:

Together there were baked sweet potato peels,

With their blackened sugar,

Among the day's cinders.

There was neither flower nor lamp,

But only that which the cold daylight allowed.

The poverty of the setting energized us,

And we waited,

With innocent press,

For the years to unfold,

And to bring us, again,

To remembrance.

Written after 1992

-Of our family in cruelest winter, in the rural

Brothers

Toes nudging into the summer day's dust,

A smile as grande as the morning;

Slender, sunny brown tones out of worn denim,

Stained of mulberry;

A small, familiar treasure

Rests in the front pocket,

The blades sitting like corn kernels

In their canoe.

-Never again, but then, all over, sonnyboy.

The way I remember some of the most gentle

and complete love that I have known

Written after 1992

Miss Beulah's in Summer

One

We always knew the evening,

A coming in,

A returning to the hearth given away to morning –

All, both cattle and fowl,

Respectful winds and fragrance bruised of warmth;

Windows and doors bore open,

Watching the falling light.

And a silence found us,

Not strange or unkind, but a familiar

Song of absence and kept thought,

Opened into its full bouquet,

Furnishing still another time of sweet together,

With friends of acceptance and praise,

With an ambiance provided

In the gentle smoke of night,

The day fire having burned,

Bringing in its dying coals,

Promise of tomorrow.

-At Miss Beulah's: the "house place" at which we lived

Before leaving the rural-

Written in 2001

Miss Beulah's in Summer

Two

Holy Father God,

Hear my petition, that not ever let

The knowing that can be mine alone,

Go away from me,

These my little slender,

Summer brown skin hearts,

To not ever go away from me,

These whose laughter sounds

In the selected yet,

A tea, the bright scarlet of innocent love,

To drink and refresh the present, of its past,

This that grew a compassion in me,

Requiring a sword that I wish,

In the converse of its full strength, to strike true.

Let them come to me, over and again,

Wading the stream of the day,

And when the night, let their images,

And all that these of beauty surpassing,

Touching even now,

Summer into the haunting dream of September,

Echoes that sound the distant bell –

These may offer such to me,

To let this joy flow

Over my eyes in their closing.

March Prayer, 2001

Lord have mercy, Lord have mercy, Lord have mercy;

Great thanksgivings, and blessings grant to those I love,

Here and apart,

And for all who feel helpless and alone.

Miss Buleah's comes again to me, in every day,

But especially at prayers;

Our innocence,

Of then, never to be regained,

For we were souls new to our light,

In it unfamiliar so that we did not see its lessening

As we took on more our mortal selves.

-A prayer for our family, the tragedy of our love together,

With combined elements of the liturgy from Episcopal and

Russian Orthodox orders of service_

-In October of 2002, our family experienced a schism, I, my brothers and their families,

Growing since our parents' deaths, and has not been repaired, acceptably

Part Song

The morning-glory opened her blue eyes;

Bright red feathers fell gracefully,

Almost to earth,

And then, just as gracefully,

Lifted swiftly to the sky.

The moving sunset hues brushed in pebbles of brightness;

<u>The earth gave up her fresh fragrance to us</u>

<u>As we stood up to our knees</u>

<u>In the newly watered earth, and laughed.</u>

Quickly, before it goes,

I smile, securely, feeling, perhaps,

Life is not happenchance.

Early 1970's

Of my brothers, my little "brown skins"

-an old memory, very old, probably ages

Part Song

Driving yesterday morning-

Cree myrtle bushes with blossoms like large,

Red watermelon halves;

And puddles, from the rain the night before

Riding the sun's rays into the upper blue,

Leaving spider-webby places –

And I saw bare foot tracks there.

Written in the early 1970's

Reaching Into

"A Dream and Some Embroidery"

-   A short story, written in seventh grade, at age twelve (1952)

Which won first prize of a school writing contest ($20.00);

I purchased my first pair of "high heeled" shoes,

And Mamma had me return them.

The piece has been lost.

Dancer

Graceful, dark-eyed, Russian girl,

With your long and fleecy curls –

What sadness fills your heart tonight,

That blocks our your soft and graceful light

...for as you swing and sway and prance,

To this old folk Russian dance,

Let new joy within enfold,

Into your heart...sad and cold...

About\near 1958

"Dancer:" a verse written in the years between the eleventh and twelfth grades
of high school, (1957-58) showing grave symptoms of depression.

The piece is a fragment.

Excerpts from " Homefires "

(S h o r t S t o r y T r i l o g y)

Singing at the little church always inspired me.

It was slow, often giving the impression of no rehearsal,

But always strong, meaningful,

Full of devotion.

The view outside was equally as enjoyable –

Lovely woods and sunlight,

Dogs lying in the sun,

The sound of birds in the quietness of prayers.

A fresh green voile dress trimmed with pearl buttons

Could not have been lovelier that the scene that appeared

Through the small church windows.

...Suddenly, without introduction, I saw the tree –

Red, crimson, standing just inside a fence,

Not quite as tall as the oak in whose shadow it stood.

It was perfectly shaped, very nearly the triangle children draw

When they first discover trees.

The leaves were like blood,

Becoming black at the points where they were attached

In clusters to various limbs.

These leaves had the quality of fine satin in the evening sunlight:

I had not seen the tree before;

Indeed I had seen none of the trees but now, as I looked,

I saw that they were there,

In all colors, making innumerable patterns against

The background of the sky.

Written at age 23-24

Immediately before becoming ill, and leaving college instruction

Sweet Oblivion

Except for these, sweet oblivion:

The exquisite, ballerina-like beauty of the butterfly;

The poignant fragrance of the fading rose;

The graceful movements of a field of golden rod,

Like yards and yards of flowing yellow organza;

And the soft fantasias the snowflakes can form –

Except for these, and that whole part of me

That needs them,

I would choose –

Sweet oblivion, and then, still,

My secret self would weep for its lost part.

At Ms. Walden's, Jackson, MS

Written before 1970

The Struggle

I feel, sometime, that the most agonizing battles ever fought

Are those of the early morning hours,

When the known, familiar self, in the act of waking,

Comes dangerously close to the most inner self;

It is then that the old adversaries of will and circumstance

Face each other as numerous thoughts.

--"Rise, go to the warm demanding light,

Promising, but threatening;"

--"Stay, hold to the cool, undemanding darkness,

Nothingness, but protective."

To leave the familiar, and to go to the only partially known,

To continue still, rather than to change,

Over, and over, and over—the battle is always done, finished;

After moments of very personal struggle, we act, timorously,

On our decisions.

At Ms. Walden's, Jackson, MS

Written before 1970

Decision

On occasion, when I allow my thoughts to wander,

Unstructured,

My glance skirts the room...

And then I feel Achilles' pain;

It begins with a day and covers a portion of time,

Extending back through weeks, years, all passed.

For those moments, briefly,

The safety of reason and strength of defenses leave me,

Open to feel—

I struggle with youth and our common foe –

The great unavoidable compromise,

Life with no complete pureness, no secure absolutes.

Late 1960's

-At Ms. Walden's, Jackson, MS

January 2, 1969

Today was a good day for me with you –

Not because of New Year cheer –

For the weather was cold rain, and the traffic was heavy,

And the time was only the space measured

By the movement of the clock hands around their path, once.

It was not the greeting – the politeness was merely familiar;

Neither were beginning remarks more than response –

Like courtesies often exchanged.

But your first smile (the deep, polished brown of your eyes smiled too)

Was like an invitation to a sparkling wine,

Red and sweet with accepting,

Stimulating and satisfying with savoring.

In conversation, I felt a oneness,

Communication that home fires –

Sincerity in friendship, agony in speculation –

Even the coming together with a lover has not given.

Listening eyes and quietness were like soft caresses which called forth

Myself through voice, giving sounds to thoughts long

Building frustration with their silence.

Careful responses filled spaces between man and me,

And I sang on, holding fast to words perceived as strong, accepting arms.

I sang with such exhilaration that my secret parts asked for

Conscious expression, secret parts which have been known

To me only by fear felt at experiencing awareness.

So well sang I that I walked through your door to the more

Perplexing reality, thus so because my self just sung

Must again wear silence, but nonetheless I walked,

Somewhat freer, somehow, now more complete –

And all in the time which was the space measured by the movement

Of clock hands around their path, just once –

(And in that time you stooped to tie your shoe and swore!)

Of Dr. Sutton, first psychiatrist of 22 years

Companion piece behind "The Seduction Effacate" written some years later

The Seduction Effacate

The room was wrapped in hospital gauze,

And I sat in my maiden white gown at the foot of the bed;

He stood, tall,

Resting his left hand on the rail.

It was a beautiful olive, Jacob hand,

The fingers of medium length and well-formed,

Tended but purposeful.

And I asked, taking his hand,

"Are you married?"

And he answered, "What difference could it make?"

There began the long, quiet, impotent seduction,

The seduction effacate in its desert,

That my growth was in time

Fertile toward strength.

And so I think today of a Beethoven romance.

Of Dr. Sutton, my supreme benefactor- regarding a life with career, marriage and such- On the first night of hospitalization with Bipolar illness, 1965; the companion piece to January 2, 1969, was composed almost twenty years later.

-he, of love, as a woman can, in every way,

Love beyond the mere mortal, for still now twelve years,

And I continue.

November 12, 2002

The Singer

His eyes were like glazed chestnuts

When his glance fell questioningly on me;

The visiting room of the ward was small,

Not very well decorated, and always under the

Careful watch of the dull attendant.

But his carriage, as he moved toward me,

Had lost none of its grace,

Even in the state's clothes, loose grey-stripped coveralls

In which he carried all of his personal possessions:

His toothbrush and his one letter.

He did not remember me that day except,

Perhaps, as a far away glimpse,

Not the play-reading at which we had met.

His reality had been reduced to a small, locked ward

Where poor wretches lived out their illnesses or lives.

That I was there, however, that I had asked to see him,

Spoken his name –

That I was accepting of the him I would see –

His reality had been made larger;

He regained some of his old confidence

And once again he sang:

"You have brought the world in to me –

Beautiful blue wool to see;

Soft burgundy suede to touch;

Bright, ripe fruit to eat;

And the scarf from your hair –

There is a whole lifetime in its fragrance.

The difference in the beauty of his song,

And the grey world into which the words fell,

Was so much that I wanted to scream injustices

And pull down about me the poor draperies.

But I did not; I could not,

Else I could not leave freely and tie again

The scarf about my hair;

And so- I walked away that day unhappily,

Not so tall, I think, as the singer.

Before 1969

Working at the state mental hospital at Whitfield, MS –

-"The Singer," a new acquaintance who became ill with Paranoid
Schizophrenia, and was brought for treatment

My First Haiku

I saw the sun set today,

A brilliant orange pearl floating

Gracefully in the cold grey-white

Lace of clouds.

Written in the early 1970's

Return

The black slim arms in starched khaki

Held the heavy bag as he moved along the roadside,

Walking with familiarity, expectancy, joy –

Toward home, home in the early fall.

The man-child could not hide his love and eagerness;

And, after leaving him, when I tried to hum

The song with the radio, I couldn't –

My throat was tight and my heart felt big,

And full, with understanding.

1969-1971

Written during the period of the Vietnam War;

While returning home from classes, I saw a young, black soldier walking on

The roadside, with his bag, my young brother, David, serving in the marines

In Vietnam at that time.

Old House Places

I like old house places; they are like photographs of memories.

For me, borders are early spring sunsets and daffodils,

Scattered, pattern less,

Down banks from once, well-kept beds.

Highlights and focal points always include

A broken dish, blue,

Covered partially with earth –

And just a way off, rust and iron,

Old farm implements, made almost pretty by lilies

Beginning another cycle of buds and blossoms and leaves.

There are nails and broken glass and grey, old wood –

But, almost always, standing on a rise,

Is the monument to past life – the hearth –

Place, the chimney – formidable, awesome,

And a little bittersweet in decay.

Finally, a last glimpse will find, to the right,

Just at the edge, a peach tree,

Standing as if someone had spilled black ink on the picture,

Forming trunk, limbs, twigs;

And the rarest spot of all –

Where one of the jagged limbs plucked out of the soft,

Pink sunset clouds – its first blossom.

Before 1970

Second version

Old House places

I like old house places,

Easily distinguished from the countryside

By cedar or magnolia trees, planted neatly in a row,

Or, more often by chimneys, partially crumbled,

Sometimes alone or in pairs, opposite each other,

As were the rooms they warmed,

Probably separated by an open hall.

Often lilies, daffodils and other spring flowers cover the bank

Or ditch in the front of the house place,

Washed there from well-worked beds,

In the clean, swept yard.

On closer examination, one finds, now, useless fences,

A broken cup, or enamel pot and almost always

There is a flowering quince bush, a variety of fruit trees,

Beautiful in bloom;

And most important, crepe myrtle trees,

Pink like melons and soft in clusters.

I like old home places because in identifying them

I dream stories of the life once there, and then

They are beautiful to me,

Perhaps all the more so because they are gone for I,

Without exception- grieve for, <u>and hold dear</u>,

<u>That which is past.</u>

-The first version of this poem, written very early, before 1970, but
holding, still, a sentiment which is a true part of me

Today's Treasures

Today was over and I had thought it

Hardly a day at all; the morning had come

And the time moved into sunset. But in

My loneliness I now smiled because I could carry

Into the night treasures to tuck away

And be my company:

The last hibiscus – a morning discovery,

Crimson red, soft and feathery;

A full-blown peace rose with

Yellow petals outlined by pale pink veins,

Barely visible in the evening light;

And finally, the oak leaves – I saw them

From the breakfast room when they

Were surrounded with sunlight,

Shiny like syrup, a rich, beautiful

Burnt-red color,

Reminiscent of the Mediterranean sand,

Said by the proud Romans to always

Be blown into their city when rain comes.

Composed in the early 1970's

The Splash of Red

They grey sky drifted down between all of the bare

Grey branches of the trees, bare except

For long flowing beards of grey moss

Which reached back into the sky,

Completing the circle.

In the moving fog, the evergreens, mostly pines,

Appeared muted in color,

And the cold earth, the roadside,

Paths and banks, were flesh-color,

Not pretty with surface lights,

But old and silent, rudy and tired.

I continued on into the grey world because

The road carried me there;

The world inside me was grey too.

That I was not the first to face adversity,

That I was not the first to experience sorrow,

That hopelessness did not rise and fall within me alone –

All comforted me very little. But the Bird did:

An unexpected, small moving splash of red

Pulled the grey out of me

And the grey outside away from me.

A redbird for an hour –

A redbird for an hour –

Something beautiful –

To awaken old feelings of life, good life,

Wanted life;

As it flew away into the grey,

It was still beautiful,

Even through the tears.

January 29, 1972

The Matter of Goldenrod

Today I saw some golden rod,

Or ragweed, if you please;

A field of captive sunshine

Atop a skyline green with leaves.

And I dance with sunbeams and their shadow partners;

I press the powder of the goldenrod to my face as I move

Through their sea of green into a garden of memories so sweet

That I push them back to keep the hurt away.

Excerpts from a first attempt at verse-

Having moved to Jackson, after, becoming ill, 1967

Part-song

Home night sounds

And wind in trees like great fans

Make me feel that all I am,

Feel, be – is what was,

And I stumble alone in the aftertime.

Late 1960's

Having met and entered the relationship with my second husband, Richard-

Part-song

Clouds move,

And with just one glance,

Always, seemingly, in one direction,

In numerous patterns and thicknesses,

Unhappily, like people,

Forming a huge, grotesque collage.

Early 1970's

The Promise That Became Silent

Summertime Wind

Summertime wind is often constant

And all outdoors dances with it,

Or else it is terribly quiet and we succumb

To feelings of pressure,

From deep within or to the full pores of our warm skin.

And if it blows constant,

It can, strangely so, appear like fall,

Off away when the sun

Is slowly removing itself,

And things are dying.

Just after re-marriage in 1970

Richard away; I remember; while sunbathing-

Geraniums

I watched the geraniums move in the wind,

And heard the chimes sound above me;

Far into myself I saw

High priestess dressed in red,

Ringing small bells.

It was a soft time, a quiet time,

And I worshipped silently

At this beauty shrine.

Written in first year of marriage to Richard, 1970's

Mirrors

In today's evening hours,

I gathered honeysuckle and roses;

To complete, I added jasmine.

When I placed them in my room,

Their fragrance embraced me

Like a rich, warm oil.

For a moment,

I left the world of shape and form;

I was sunshine and I was flower;

I was early morning freshness

And the stillness of the afternoon's denouement.

I escaped the men and the time of stone and glass –

And then my glance fell upon the hanging mirrors;

With heavy grief,

I saw only my reflection,

A young matron woman,

Lost, holding a bouquet of freshly cut flowers.

July 27, 2009

Old pieces, hurriedly written, now brought out to be recorded-

These pieces were written in troubled times, with illness not well controlled –

My First Morning-glory

Early today, I went to see my first morning-glory;

It was fresh as dew, and blue as the blue sky.

It was precious as I held it,

For it pulled out of me shadows of several years.

There is enough of the past in today

That I need not wear its darkness all time,

Nor is the future threatening so

That I should constantly seek out covering.

I must paint today's sunsets,

Trace the veins of the living blossoms,

For today...

July 27, 2009

Written in first year of marriage to Richard, 1970's

Brought out later to be recorded

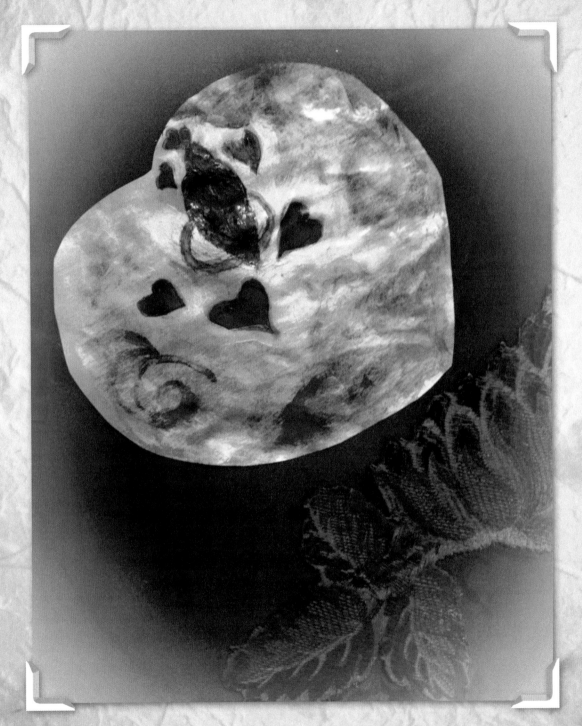

The Wall

Deep, red garnet stones

And promises near Valentine's Day,

All mixed with scornful words and looks of complete contempt

At my "feigned" weakness;

A slight kiss for my warm cheek,

Followed by reproaches and sharp instructions –

Long hours of painful silence

Conclude with a quick, dutiful embrace,

And then obscenities.

Am I too sensitive?

But that is where I meet the wall;

The "sensitive I" is me.

And so – how am I to care?

Of Richard, 1971

Again

Today had been Easter Sunday,

And, innocently enough,

I let it leave me still more alone.

"Bring some honeysuckle from behind the fence."

"Why?"

"Because it so smells like Easter!"

"Oh – I didn't know Easter smelled."

--Again, I faced the wall.

Of Richard, 1971

Summerlude

This summer is fast becoming an interlude,

A warm, lovely period into which

I casually eased, and enjoyed,

Knowing, all the while,

That it would soon pass.

Your wild plums have fallen into a cascade

Of orange shadings, fading into earthtones,

Giving up a fragrance akin to the bouquet of a fine, old brandy.

The fields of golden rod are now all about the countryside,

A bright, golden thread in the colorful tapestry that fall weaves –

And so, I know, well, it passes.

But then, this is not my first "interlude;"

All of my years have given me one –

And I will store this one, as I have all of the others,

With a special wrapping,

This year, a pleasant memory.

The three oaks will be there, longtime, I think,

Outside the breakfast room –

And so, long, I will have my memory.

I found myself a place, early in the easy days.

Very carefully put into the earth were eight morning-glory seeds,

And, up from the earth came eight morning-glories!

And so- I felt the place favored, the eight plants a good omen.

Everyday I have watched the spot,

Taking a few moments for my very own.

My silvery and very stately friend went with me early

In the mornings to leave bread beneath the oaks for the birds.

He ate some of our gifts,

But most often restrained himself,

And, with his own grace,

Ran about with his magnificent tail curled on his back,

Or danced with damp feet, on mine.

The birds came and played,

Like music given color.

Oranges, yellows, and browns met blues sprinkled

With white and grey – and they all bowed gracefully away,

For those dressed in red.

The mourning dove in the first hours became more distant,

And finally, the whippoorwill would begin his wood song-

Until the next morning time –

And I still had my place.

Each time my glance fell on it,

I felt a good feeling,

The memory I am putting away –

Some excitement and pleasure

At sunrise and a small gathering

Of peace and satisfaction at sunset.

1970's

Of L.

Morning time

Love, when I waked this morning,

All was still dark outside

And I thought you must be waking, too.

When I went to the door,

I felt the air, fresh and cool and damp –

Like when you're working in summer

And rise to feel the wind touch your wet body.

And, love, today, driving out,

I saw all the many shadings

In the trees that line the road,

Giving a preview of the splendor

Their harvest of color will soon bring.

I saw the first red lily,

Beautiful only in its blossom,

Always a surprise,

Because it never shows until, you know,

One day in beginning fall

-There it stands on a tall, leafless stem,

Sometimes alone,

Or in scattered groupings.

Also I saw persimmon trees,

Many it seemed,

More than anytime since I was little girl,

And the limbs bent heavily

With their many, lovely cadmium, orange-red jewels.

And I must not forget the golden rod

Gracefully draping the road

And dancing with beautiful coordination in the wind.

I'm glad you told me about

The handsome fox, and the small rabbit,

And the summer grapes;

Though they brought bittersweet thoughts

From the laces of memory,

They prompted me

To see other threads of old times,

Pleasant ones,

And think of you.

1970's

Of L.

Our Now

When we sat together last night,

And watched the spider weave from the rose,

And smiled into the moonlight,

The softness of the rose petals

The quietness of the spider's weaving,

The brightness of the moon –

All came together in your touch,

The kisses you playfully took from your lips

And put behind my ear with your finger,

And the smile in your eyes that covered me completely –

So that for that time,

That space,

I felt, and did not think;

There were no shadows –

Only now, and now, and now.

1970's

Of W.

Reunons Nous

The sun has come and splashed his brightness

On my natursum bed so many mornings now

That it has taken on the appearance

Of a box of jewels –

Or perhaps the colors left on the artist's palate:

Red and orange and yellow and gold.

The moon has spilled silver through my window,

Too many nights!

And I have gone to the gate to admire

My third morning-glory of the season, so often,

That I can almost feel its freshness as I write,

See its fine burgundy blossom,

With veins as perfect as those

Lining the pale breast of a very fair lady.

The fireflies have come and teased me in the early evening hours,

With their tiny sparkling's of colored light

As the night sounds ended my days.

Nature, longtime my close companion,

Has marked well the hours since your tenderness

Covered me completely. Come to me soon;

Let the Grande Old Dame smile,

In her varied fashions, on our togetherness!

(1970's – a lover- not seen for some time- I do not, now, remember)

Tribute

She went away today;

Her eyes were closed and dark,

Her nose straight and lovely,

Her mouth, truest gentle,

And her hands, with thumbnails, like long,

Slim, perfect ovals;

I have seen those ovals in Her first born,

And then in her last born.

I turned and left Her when

I thought of the saga of those hands.

But I will not soon forget.

There will never be fragrant honeysuckle in spring,

Warm, dusty days outside a wooden, yard fence in summer,

Sprawling chrysanthemums in fall,

Or the taste of chocolate in winter-

That I will not think of her

And hold her softly to my heart.

Of my maternal grandmother, 1970's

Fall time

It is fall time now,

And all about me is golden;

But I seem to think, still,

Of summer and rose tones.

I went home in the summer,

Really home,

So far into home time

I went that my soul

Almost found its beginning place.

And I did want to stay –

For it was with coming toward now

That the excursion took on

A bittersweet quality.

Of home, parents in Wesson, MS

A later verse

Passing Seasons

-Soft, crepe myrtle florets

Left-over summer,

Falling into a bed of newly come,

Bright chrysanthemums –

Ah, autumn, more,

Seasons passing each other.

-a part song, later or last of the verses of early 1970's

-early Hinds years

People forming a huge collage –

So there it is – a glimpse of life,

Like Shelley's dome of many colors.

It is I, too, ever moving, and with reflection,

In a known way – except I wonder –

Am I well formed – square, round, nebulous,

And how does the light fall on me today –

Unhappy reflection – bright, dark, shaded-

But most, the agony-filled question:

Constant?

-A thought written while alone at Pineview Drive, in Clinton, MS, Richard away traveling; the fragment shows the symptomatic nature of my troubled thought, at that time of just re-marriage- a part-song – one of few such recorded – early 1970's, my inside knowing of my tenuous hold – (constant or well, or broken, ill)

And Still the Moment," *Seasonal Portions*

Emitting from a large bowl of apples,

Near the cornered, hall doorway, was a fragrance,

Quite the small candle in a darkened area,

Its fingers of light touching my soul with gentle refreshment.

A portion of pain came in a familiar poignancy,

That apples had appeared, first, in childhood's laughter,

With my "brown skins" about, and had died –

As the lighted candle would,

As the crimson fragrance must – in unkind circumstance.

And, still, the moment – beautiful and sweet, bringing the lost joy inside the pain-

It was, yet, and I reached for it, eagerly, hungrily,

Knowing the satisfaction of beautiful days with summer showers:

Ah, again, Sarto – there strikes another balance.

September 25, 2012

Conclusion

Myths, and most of the thought constellations which draw them, for a short period, or indefinitely, are sad. They are beautiful, often, with many particulars, which they gift to us, but, without help, they can, and do, metaphorically, draw their own demise. However, such words are not final, and there are occasions, more less than often, in which the myth, the dream becomes, in some measure, a reality; such is an individual reality, a personal reality seen through, most, the perspective system of the individual seer, the "knower," But, again, less often than more, an even wider audience becomes "aware," seeing:" the myth into being – and therein lies the glory of us "lesser gods" – will becomes champion to circumstance. Yet the being of myth is just, finally, less – mortal – almost always as per recorded, imperial evidence, and will knows a span of life.

Hopefully, these properties of the myth into being, and ultimately into loss – these do not most, crowd our attention in the matter's entire. However, if we do forget, and if our attention wanders toward fullest truth, we must join with the nineteenth century, French poet, Paul Verlaine, in his work (verse) "Chanson d' Autumne" ("the tears of Autumn," describing the coming close, in all of its beauty: "et je pleure": and I weep.

Pity, aside, and reason to the fore, I am aware of the circumstances of my being, not in principle different from all other, but in the degree of experiencing, somewhat overmuch, perhaps, I have, since early childhood, repeatedly "loved and lost," moment by moment, at times, losing the day in "pressing importances." And in the pain, I have repeatedly found a balm through the medium of beauty, to often, then, in gratitude, create other beauty as expression of that gratitude.

These humble expressions comprise my work, the earliest being in painting, music, and floral with tapestry design together with others, sewing, sculpting later, alongside enjoying friendship and entertainment, at various levels as well as the "bliss of solitude." Since young adulthood (age twenty) I have found my true bliss in instructing able, insightful college students in the areas of Psychology and Literature. But my primary mode of expression, writing, began as a pubescent child, while composing in the seventh grade. I have written, most in the genre of poetry, but also, considerably, in prose, or prose verse. In the main, my poetry is written in blank free verse.

There is no antidote to truth, but only to recognize and embrace that of it which enlarges, comforts, and offers to others.   And so, my life, described from earliest images of the myth I somehow knew could be in place – until the "silence," to then a, now, flowering- has become to me a "thing of beauty," a "being" of light and dark, culminating in a feast of, often, joy; nevertheless, as I reflect on the struggle, and the exhilaration in conquering, I know that such is mortal joy, and with/on that knowledge, I repeat the refrain, "et je pleure."

-Ought but to re-examine Mr. Keats, and his particular statement in the much loved work, "Endemyion:" "A thing of beauty is a joy forever; its loveliness increases, it will never pass into nothingness." If we attempt and resolve the dissonance of its wisdom and "objective realities;" such becomes, of necessity, a very personal arrangement, more a deep and abiding acceptance; this present work is record to the latter idea formulation.

Elizabeth

Inside winter thought, 2014

Comment

I have begun with my earliest impressions, and part-songs, recorded only in the years of my late twenties, the years which saw my second marriage and perhaps the second most disordered period of my illness – to the degree that all forms of expression, including writing, were discontinued. This period extended past twenty years. Representative thought from my earliest period of expression constitutes the body of this work, *The Myth of Being.* It is written in free verse, as is the greater portion of my compositions, although there is some good amount of prose. Since I was a student of literature, I have felt that arriving at truth – in writing to offer information, inspiration, agreement and responsibility, entertainment, and beauty with wisdom – these are more easily accomplished – without concern with form. Emphasis rests in content, rather than structure, allowing energies to be free of great restrictions, to be used with more worthy endeavor. And although some portion of beauty may be left unattended, if the poet *feels* his words, a "natural" cadence will provide to his thought. The illustrations and cover are also from these earliest years, memory given color and form; acrylic paints, including metallics, pearl, and crystals are employed, ink pens helping with the finer details. Added, somewhat sparingly, are "finger tip" glazes which do not require firing: the subjects, poignant images carried these years, appearing, at times, too intense, since they are touched, still, with great love, and loss.

Time is, and in its isness, kind and unkind.

The blossoms we gather, arrange both lovely, and lovely, less;

Through perception, alone,

They become, if cultivated,

The thoughts that fulfill in the worlds

Of our separate realities, existence in its wholeness,

The full myth of being.

Breath, sighs, tears –

Shadow, prayers, hope, sentiment, travail –

Echoes, mists, and whispers –

These, all, compiled, throughout, and chorus

At full achievement, of presence, being –

Out of myth, the annunciation of truest freedom.

My Firelighter

Brightly colored threads

Wind their way through a tapestry of love;

Some are the showing of golden rod and morning-glories,

Or being invited to eat a ripe fig, fresh from the tree;

But now, as summer gives into fall,

I see one thread that shines more brightly.

A little girl who saw dragons

And other creatures in the dark of moonless winter nights,

I looked longingly at the one,

Roughed in window of the cold bedroom

Where I slept with my three brothers.

All I needed was a little light to chase away the monsters.

But it was bedtime

And oil for the lamp was dear;

Enough wood for fires was difficult to find and gather.

And then Mamma would open the door to her room,

Which was also the fireplace room;

Somehow she would find enough pieces

To build again a small fire from the glowing coals.

When the fire was burned,

I was asleep, saved again,

By my gentle firelighter.

1990's

Of Mamma

Giving Strength

Mozart and the clarinet:

His smile of full lips softly curved

In unaccustomed gentleness;

Papa, Papa,

You do not stay long enough,

For my heart would willingly burst

With your full presence.

Instead, images of fields, dusty roads,

The ax and the plow,

A fellowship with the seasons

Shape, with care, my memory

Of giving strength.

My heart does not burst,

But rather assumes the posture

Of having tasted a sweetmeat

Dressed in reverent, but bitter herbs.

Of my father,

A sharecropper who took his family back to school (college) and ministry

easter/2003

sine scripta (in fear of splendid day)

where did all the little girls go — into the away,
perhaps, a forever, far away?
Once a little girl who embraced
play, and laughter, and willing, healing
sleep.
there were thoughts, but they have died into time;
little girl — no more, revealing to
this may's second smile,
only inside a tear, and it is lost, alas,
on the face of another, further away,

I slept, into the long, spring afternoon, a great,
long time, it seemed, for no one knew,
and no one looked beyond
the two white rosebuds, their farewelling in
their becoming,
beautiful beginnings, the till day —
but, oh, the day, so quickly its flourish,
and opened for fullness, the innocent
giving of the flower
to the generous taking of the sun:
how soft, how masterful, how sad, and
all the bells of the meadow,
in their ringing,
say so.

colors fly by, their music leaving their rainbow
while I cannot hold them.
and so,

- 101 -

they become a paint, familiar,
and I, less than I was;
Jason horse, beauty horse, strength riding
away,
and the little death will know where
my all are, were,
fancy, fancy, away.

the first day of school, or perhaps the last day —
crepe myrtle in fragile, southern rose,
to offer to the little quietened white
shirt.

Why do we know, why do we keep — when all is
to fall into the great womb of ever:
becoming — something other, other than
we are, we were, we knew —

There is no picture to my life, only a flower resting
atop a fine horse who has steel, yet magnificent
titanium in his right, front leg,
this glory, she, the flower rode.
I have woven a tale, and it knows a true beginning,
but its heart passed, always,
Among receiving others, yet those
receiving, knowing their grace, these as sand grains.
legion, as summer leaves, and raindrops, the
flowing scarf of sunlight —
these, so that a mist of fatigue, with what is, was her
unkind conqueror, and his sword, at her neck.

*grave
receptive
with my entirety
immediate family
especially my nephew
of soul —
one year
and more, now.

"little night"
death

*my
heart of
true wisdom

her arms choosing
not to cross for such mercy,

was permitted
its thrust,
granting its mercy.

elizabeth
may 2-3, 2003

Reflections of us children, and as adults, in our nuclear, and extended families, later, one year past the formal break, October, 2002.

Other works by Elizabeth Clayton

I, Elizabeth
2007

Songs from the Eleventh Month
2008

A Thousand White Gardenias
2009

Unto Relationship
2009

Musings
2009

La libellule
2010

Chanson de Harold
2011

Shenandoah Songs
2012

The Sun and Geranium Poems
2012

Scarlet Flow
2012

Seasonal Portions
2013

Printed in the United States
By Bookmasters